Mental and Financial Growth

BUSINESSFITNESSHELP

Copyright © 2020 BusinessFitnessHelp

All rights reserved.

ISBN:

This document is geared towards providing exact and reliable information in regards to the topic and issue covered. The publication is sold with the idea that the publisher is not required to render accounting, officially permitted or otherwise qualified services. If advice is necessary, legal or professional, a practiced individual in the profession should be ordered.
Under no circumstance will any legal responsibility or blame be held against the publisher for any reparation, damages, or monetary loss due to the information herein, either directly or indirectly.

Legal Notice:
The book is copyright protected. This is only for personal use. You cannot amend, distribute, sell, use, quote, or paraphrase any part of the content within this book without the consent of the author.

Disclaimer Notice:
Please note the information contained within this document is for educational and entertainment purposes only. Every attempt has been made to provide accurate, up to date, and reliable complete information. No warranties of any kind are expressed or implied.
Readers acknowledge that the author is not engaging in the rendering of legal, financial, medical, or professional advice. The content of this book has been derived from various sources. Please consult a licensed professional before attempting any techniques outlined in this book.
By reading this document, the reader agrees that under no circumstances are is the author responsible for any losses, direct or indirect, which are incurred as a result the use of information contained within this document, including, but not limited to, errors, omissions, or inaccuracies.

CONTENTS

Introduction	1
Mental Growth	3
Mental Exercises to Make You a Better Critical Thinker	16
The Lost Art of Independent Thinking	20
Financial Freedom	30
Approaching Risk	49
Open-Mindedness	56
Intense Intent	59
Positive Thinking Can Help With Mental And Financial Growth	65

INTRODUCTION

In basic terms, the idea of personal growth is that you improve actively as an individual, changing your life psychologically and financially on a daily basis. Mental and financial growth is a vital part of life because it gives you the ability to learn new experiences and an incentive for you to improve as a person. It is particularly relevant in today's culture that we work for our personal growth. The universe around us is going far quicker than before and our own physical or moral needs can quickly be overlooked as we seek to deal with the turmoil that is around us.

Personal growth will, however, be critical for your wellbeing in this harsh environment and your progress. You will face the obstacles that life poses to you more physically, emotionally and financially. Often, you can make changes for people nearest to you as you consistently focus on enhancing yourself as a human. This means you will not only better yourself, but also draw on the relationships you have with others, by prioritizing your own professional growth.

This growth isn't a short to medium-term cycle. This is an ongoing cycle as well as a commitment that will allow individuals "to assess their skills, to take their goals into account and to set goals so that their potentials can be maximized." The cycle of growing up successfully as an adult can be daunting, but the perseverance you gain from attempting is one of the many valuable qualities that professional growth can create.

Personal growth in your academics and in the world of work will allow you to flourish. You can quickly transfer your talents and abilities into the business world around you by focusing on your body and mind. In reality, personal growth will give you the tools to set life goals that boost your chances for employability, increasing your motivation and enhance your quality of life.

MENTAL GROWTH

Mental growth ensures that everyday routines that build mental skills are formed. It also means giving up unhealthy habits that are stopping you from moving forward. We must develop our mental strength to evolve mentally. Mental toughness is something that individuals who want to make professional growth a priority over time must develop. Just as we can make physical gains from better work-outs and diet, we need to build good mental habits, such as appreciation if we want to see benefits in mental strength.

Likewise, for physical benefits, it is also essential that we abandon unhealthy habits, such as fast food, and abandon unhealthy behaviors for mental benefit, such as feeling sorry for oneself. We can all get mentally stronger, it's essential to exercise and strengthen your mental muscles – much as you would if you were to develop physical strength.

On Building Resilience and Mental Toughness

The term resilience is in fact borrowed from engineering and is widely used in reference to positive mental well-being. It refers to the potential of a material or entity to spring back into shape. As a structural object requires resilience and durability to bounce back, a person often needs these characteristics to be mentally resilient.

In the face of adversity, traumas, tragedy, risks or even substantial pressures, the American Psychological Association describes mental endurance as an adaptation. A related definition, mental resilience, applies to the capacity to remain stable in the face of hardship, to stay concentrated and motivated in spite of the challenges. An individual who is mentally strong looks upon obstacles and adversities as an incentive, not as a threat and has the confidence and the positive outlook to pursue.

You have to be resilient to be strong mentally, but not every resilient person is automatically mentally strong. The endurance would be the peak, as you think of it as a metaphor, while mental strength may be one of the techniques to scale this mountain.

The word "survive and succeed" is helpful as Strycharczyk talks about the distinction. Resilience lets you survive and mental strength helps you succeed. Mental strength starts as you want to recognize what happens in your head without actually knowing it. Then find the will to invoke positive feelings on the present situation.

The strategies to improve mental resilience have five elements, according to Strycharczyk and Cloughe.

- Anxiety Control

- Visualization

- Positive Thinking

- Attentional Control

- Goal Setting

Just as with building mental strength, cultivating mental resilience requires self-consciousness and dedication. In general, mentally tough people tend to reach a higher degree of happiness than mentally sensitive people.

Turner identifies four main mental strength characteristics which he calls the 4C: Commitment, Challenge, Control, and Confidence. Some of these traits can be seen, but the four attributes together are the secret to success.

The psychometric tool called MTQ48, developed by Prof. Peter Clough of Manchester Metropolitan University, is used to assess mental resilience. The MTQ48 tool, which tests critical mental toughness components, is clinically accurate and effective based on this 4C framework.

The 4 C's of Mental Toughness:

Control - It is how much you care about your life, including your feelings and the purpose of your life. Your self-esteem may be taken as the control component. Getting high on your control level means getting confident in your own skin and knowing who you are. You should regulate your feelings – less likely to show your emotional state to others - and less likely to be disturbed by other people's emotions. Being low on the control scale implies that you may feel like things are occurring and you don't have much impact.

Commitment - That is how centered and happy you are. Getting high on the Commitment scale involves being able to efficiently set and accomplish goals consistently, without disrupting oneself. A high degree of dedication indicates that you are excellent at establishing positive rituals and behaviors. If you are low on the Commitment scale, you can find it difficult to establish and formulate goals, or adjust to effective routines or behaviors indicative of success. Other things or conflicting interests will also confuse you easily.

The Control and Commitment scales combined comprise the resilience part of the concept of mental toughness. That is important, as it needs a feeling of realizing you have power of your life and will make a difference as you come back from setbacks. It also requires concentration on your desired course and the desire to develop routines and priorities.

Challenge - This is how driven and adaptable you are. You are ready to accomplish your personal best by being up in the game, and seeing obstacles, shifts and adversities as incentives and not as risks, you're definitely versatile and agile. Lowering the rate of difficulty ensures you will see progress in the face of defeat and prevent new or difficult conditions.

Confidence - That is your belief, and the assumption that you will affect others, in your capacity to be successful, productive or competent. To be high in confidence is to believe you can complete assignments effectively and take measures to reverse while retaining your routine and also improving your resolve. To be weak in terms of trust implies that you can quickly get angry and don't believe in being successful or manipulating others.

The Challenge and Confidence scales together represent the trust aspect of the concept of mental thoroughness. This ensures that we can recognize and take an opportunity and see circumstances as opportunities to welcome and pursue. That makes sense, as you are more able to turn challenges into positive results if you rely on yourself and your strengths and communicate comfortably with others.

Ways to Build and Improve Resilience

As we have discovered, it is not something agreed on at birth that you can boost your level of mental resilience, over your lifetime. There are some methods and approaches to enhance mental resilience.

Three protection techniques are proposed by Rob Whitley:

Goal Setting - The desire to pursue these goals, the ability to take initiative and succeed both leads to willpower and mental resilience. Targets may be high or low, linked to wellness, mental wellbeing, career, finance, spirituality and much more. Targets requiring the development of skills would have double advantages. Learning a foreign language or learning an instrument, for example. Some research suggests that it can be particularly beneficial to set and strive towards purposes outside the individual, i.e. religious engagement or charitable service for a cause. It will offer a greater sense of mission and attachment, which in tough times can be important.

Controlled Exposure - Controlled exposure pertains to the constructive exposure of people to anxiety-provoking conditions. Evidence suggests that it can promote persistence, especially where skill development and the setting of goals are involved-a threefold benefit. For example, public speaking is an essential talent in life, but it still makes a lot of people afraid. Individuals who dislike public speech should set goals for regulated communication to improve and gain this specific skill. You will show yourself to a limited crowd of one or two people and increase your reach over time gradually. This type of action plan may be implemented by the participant or created by a Cognitive Behavioral Therapy professional therapist. Effective practice can boost self-esteem and a feeling of control and superiority that can both be found in hardship times.

Skill Acquisition - Learning new skills can play a significant role in developing resilience, as it helps you create a sense of superiority and maturity - which can be applied both in times of challenge and also increases self-esteem and problem-solving capacity. The skills that are to be acquired depend on the person. For instance, others may benefit from enhancing cognitive ability, such as working memory or selective awareness, which helps them perform daily. Others may gain from skill-based instruction by discovering new hobbies. The development of new skills in a group setting provides social reinforcement and often fosters resilience.

The United State Psychological Association shares 11 behavioral toughness strategies:

Move toward your goals - Although formulation of long-term, big goals is crucial, it is however vital to ensure that they are practical. The creation of small, workable steps allows our targets to be accomplished and encourages us to work consistently towards these goals and to build "little wins." Try every day to take a little step toward your target.

Keep things in perspective - If times are rough, do remember that things could be worse; try to keep them from getting out of proportion. Once faced with complicated and traumatic incidents, it helps to keep a long-term outlook.

Maintain a hopeful outlook - We become less able to consider a solution as we dwell on what's wrong with the problem and stay in a frightening state. Seek to maintain a good outlook and consider the outcome to be positive rather than negative. In this respect, visualization may be useful.

Take care of yourself - Self-care is a crucial tool to create endurance and helps to sustain a balanced mind and body that tackles challenging issues when they occur. Taking care of yourself implies taking care of your own needs, feelings and activities which bring you happiness and relaxation. Frequent physical exercise is also a perfect way to take care of yourself.

Take decisive actions - Rather of shying away from challenges and pressures, hoping they would all go down, try and take decisive steps wherever possible.

Look for opportunities for self-discovery - Tragedy will also contribute to tremendous insight and growth in an individual. A tough situation will improve our trust and self-worth, enhance our relationships and teach us a lot about ourselves. Many people with disabilities have shared enhanced love of life and enhanced spirituality.

Nurture a positive view of yourself - Working to develop self-confidence may help to avoid challenges and create resilience. It is important to have a good view of yourself when solving challenges and trusting your own intuition.

Additional approaches to improve resilience can be useful - Building resilience can look to different people like different things. Paper, thanksgiving, meditation and other spiritual rituals serve to bring faith to certain people and reinforce their commitment.

Make connections - Our connection to families, friends and society will improve resilience. Healthy relationships with people who are worried about you and listen to your concerns, will help us restore optimism through tough times. Similarly, it can be very helpful for us to support others in their time of need and to foster our own sense of resilience.

Avoid seeing crises as insurmountable problems - We can't alter the ongoing circumstances surrounding us, so we can monitor our reactions. In life there will still be problems, but despite any difficult situation you face, it's important to be conscious that situations are going to change. Take note of the small ways in which the unpleasant situation will already begin to feel better.

Accept that change is a part of living - They say that change is the only consistent aspect in life. According to challenging situations, those goals can no longer be practical or achievable. This helps you to concentrate on issues over which you have power by knowing something you cannot alter.

Improving Mental Stamina

Stamina is the capacity to withstand sustained physical or intellectual actions. Mental resilience is the only hallmark attribute that helps one to survive life's adversity. It is critical to address long-term goals as well as foreseen and unforeseen difficulties, issues or traumas. Psychological resilience calls for planning, energy, perseverance and concentration.

Sometimes we make reference to elite athletes and sport teams when we discuss about fitness as both physical and emotional strength is important to this success. However, not just athletes, anyone can benefit from improved mental resilience. Although no one develops mental resilience overnight, there are 5 tips to build your mental resilience over time:

Manage Stress - Our capacity to control tension plays a significant part in the growth of mental energy. Although not all stress is negative-a driving force can be constructive stress-it impacts our bodies similarly physically. Meditation and gradual muscle relaxation are useful methods for controlling stress. It is important to know that you control and regulate your mental state and how you treat the stressor.

Think Positively - Self-confidence in one is one of the most important characteristics of a healthy mind and conviction that one should practice and take decisions. Training yourself to think optimistically and find the positive in any situation would most likely help develop mental resilience over time.

Use Visualization - Visualization is an outstanding instrument for handling uncertainty, circumstances and fear regarding results. Close your eyes and imagine a moment when a similar situation has arisen. This involves recalling the emotion, not just the image that accompanied the achievement.

Get More Sleep - It's no secret that sleeping sufficiently is important in our daily physical and mental workings. Enough sleep may lead to decisions and reaction time on the spot. Sleep is said to be adequate for seven to nine hours or more while you are carrying out physical and mental stress activities.

Plan for Setbacks - Life definitely will not always go the way we have been dreaming or planning. Instead of focusing on failure or misfortunes, it is necessary to re-center yourself and recover attention after a break. We can't influence the future events surrounding us, so we can track what we did later. It's a smart idea to have a strategy that lets you cope if things don't go as expected.

How to Get a Better, Stronger and More Confident Mind

Confidence is one of the 4Cs of mental resilience! It is one of the key factors in building resilience to maintain an optimistic self-view and develop confidence in your abilities to solve problem and rely on your instinct. So how do we develop a confident mind?

The following are healthy ways to build your confidence:

Exercise - Exercise is not only helpful to the physical body, but also to the mind. The therapeutic advantages include increased concentration, consolidation of memory, and reducing stress and anxiety. It is also said that exercise would reduce depression and improve this. Confidence is not only due to actual, tangible advantages but also to mental advantages.

Be Fearless - To follow your dreams and ambitions without fear takes a degree of faith. Conversely, it helps to develop your confidence by first plunging your head into things that frighten you. And it is easy to be depressed and scared of defeat because we set ambitious expectations for ourselves. It is necessary in these situations to gather your courage and go one step at a time.

Get Things Done - Confidence and achievement usually go hand in hand. Accomplish goals and have confidence in your ability to accomplish your objectives, while making small steps towards their objectives.

Monitor Your Progress - It is necessary to break things down into simpler and more realistic measures when moving on a goal, large or small. You find it simpler, by watching the results in real-time, to track the success and gain trust. This will measure the goals and the practical steps to accomplish them.

Do The Right Thing - Those with high trust prefer to work up to a reliable structure and make choices dependent on that, even though it's not in their best interests. This will build a more positive spirit if the actions are consistent with the higher self.

Don't Care What Others Think - It is quick to fall into the pit of worrying what people think about you, but note that what others think matters nothing in search of your dreams. It's important to remember. Develop your self- and continue to succeed, even though some may not be in agreement.

Do More Of What Makes You Happy - It allows us to enrich our lives and become our true self if we take time to take care of ourselves and do things that bring us happiness. Confidence comes as we identify ourselves with and are proud of our highest selves.

Stand-up For Yourself - Making a stance when anyone tells you can't accomplish something an efficient way to build your confidence. All too much we can eventually believe the untruthful, because they reinforce the suspicions we can hear in our minds. To foster a positive view of oneself, these pessimistic emotions will be replaced by positive ones. Try to do that if you don't believe anyone.

Follow Through - By doing what you say you're going to do, you not only earn some respect for others but also love and confidence in yourself. You will also be encouraged by the development of your follow-through skills and probably improve your relationships.

Think Long-term - We also compete for more instant pleasure for long-term satisfaction. Through making long- choices and decisions, rather than through short- comforts, we will build up our confidence. Once you consider the motivation you want to do it, you are more fulfilled on a long- basis and are more likely to achieve your own targets.

MENTAL EXERCISES TO MAKE YOU A BETTER CRITICAL THINKER

The execution of these activities or enhanced critical thinking would maximize your life and chances of success. Critical thinking is a valuable method for any career or mission. This obliges you to critically evaluate things, to sort out your perceptions and to consider it from multiple angles that will boost your imagination. Whether you are trying to find a new idea, fix a current dilemma creatively, or simply examine how and why something has gone wrong, logical thinking will lead to better outcomes.

Yet it's tough to learn to think creatively the way you know how to drive a car or ride a dragonfly. There is no step-by-step roadmap to achieve peak critical thinking. Alternatively, you will exercise your logical reasoning, much like a muscle, before it is improved over time.

Critical Thinking Drills

These activities and drills will make us a better critical thinker:

Ask other people to explain their thought processes. Talk on something you want to solve to other men. It is important to obtain diverse perspectives on ideas, but the primary goal is to consider their ways of thought. Many people have different ways of coping with the same issue so it will allow you to develop so extend the operation.

Expose yourself to new content and new creators. This is always important to introduce yourself to new forms of content and new writers outside your comfort zone. You will tell you something new on how to think any new blogger, speaker or thinker you come across, so you can pose new facts so insights through your critical thought.

Express yourself in multiple mediums. Various people have various cognitive patterns and multiple thinking patterns. You may have a clear preference for visual, auditory or kinesthetic learning, which is cool, but it is important for you to try studying in multiple media if you want to think in different directions. For examples, if you spoke loudly about a question, consider diagramming it. Seek to write down your thoughts because you have looked at maps all day. The new vision can be very revealing.

Work backward. Working on an issue backward will allow you to consider problems that you would otherwise ignore. To have a simple example of revising one text word by sentence, spelling and grammar mistakes can be more readily found. The restoration of a breakdown from end to start will allow you to resolve the actual effect of every point in the series, not start to finish.

Talk to a 6-year-old. Einstein once said: "if you can't explain it simply, you don't understand it enough." The point of the quotation, irrespective of who says it, is relevant; it is an indicator that you have complete comprehension of the question and a way to view it in a particular context to clarify an interesting idea in plain terms. Try speaking to a 7-year-old about the concern (real or imaginary). You may discover easily aspects of the topic that you don't understand entirely and that begin to think anew about the issue.

Understand and challenge your biases. Each one of us has a variety of cognitive biases, some influencing our beliefs and some influencing our way of thought. It may be useful to identify and question these implicit differences. For instance, you should actively look for proof that is contradictory to your core theory because you believe you are influenced by confirmatory discrepancies.

Experiment with brain teasers and ethical dilemmas. Actual ethical dilemmas are still a challenge for experts, but imaginary ethical dilemmas (and other brain teasers) should be used to improve and recruit your critical thinking skills. For instance, you need to talk about the importance of life and the effect of behavior on decision-making and remorse. Most brain teasers recommend that you work "outside of the box" to tackle it properly. It's a great challenge.

One of the best exercises you can do to enhance your critical thinking is not to exercise; it is to change your environment. You will be open to more knowledge and insights and have access to much better solutions - whether your solutions are someone else's ones - because you are surrounded by logical thinkers who openly share their views and opinions. Look at those who have clear signs of disappointment before you are looking to recruit or develop a team. Otherwise, begin looking for critical thinkers online, in a peer group or in the job community.

THE LOST ART OF INDEPENDENT THINKING

We have to face and experience discomfort if we want to succeed. The vast majority of people do whatever they can to stop it, far from courting pain. This is not because people fear shifting – most want to alter every part of their life – this is just that they are unable to embrace the pressure that often comes with alter, particularly good changes. Therefore more people prefer to leave things as they are instead of coping with discomfort. And since discomfort is an important component of personal growth, this ability to escape pain means that most individuals are not able to do so.

A group's culture is defined by the values and behavior of its leaders. We addressed in previous chapters how important it is to meet individuals who both respect your goals and aspire to accomplish their own goals. This will encourage us to engage in a culture that promotes development. And, since the majority of people choose to live in their comfort zone, the everyday atmosphere of the people around you is initially highly likely to allow you to remain in the comfort zone. Obviously, this will start to change with your success, but you are usually part of a culture which deliberately and unintendedly deters growth at first.

A collective desire to stay in the comfort zone leads to a culture which gives us the illusion that safe play is better and that we aspire for a simple life. This also means that the condition is your own obligation as we agree that everyone will improve themselves and change their lives. Most people do not want to embrace this obligation. Most people are often uncomfortable because other people's acts warn them that they have not reached their true potential. We are therefore frequently in circumstances where the dominant ethos is that with diminished priorities and encouraged mediocrity.

It takes tremendous intellectual discipline to think independently from the audience. When most of you aspire to daily life, it takes bravery and a deep self-confidence to believe individually, to break away from the crowd and to follow the less-traveled path. You should not then be shocked if it is often criticized or maybe even construed as beyond your position to set your targets and then aspire to achieve them.

In the distant past, it was necessary to ensure that while people lived in limited hunter-gatherer communities, they all had precisely the same values and worldviews. You needed the support, assistance and protection of the small group of individuals around you if you were to stay alive. The group should therefore promote cohesion, deter any independence attempts and make an effort to ensure everyone understood their position. If the group determines that you don't represent the group's best interests, they will extradite you from the community. The group's inability to agree may very well be catastrophic, at a time when you wanted a group to survive. People discovered easily that social recognition is crucial to their existence. In fact, one generation to the next was aggressively trained to maintain the cohesion of the nation. This tradition of conformity has been a long-standing and long-standing custom. Of example, circumstances are today very different, so it is doubtful that they will prove fatal. Conformity is, however, still promoted, resulting in the perception that it will not be tolerated among the majority of citizens.

If we are on the verge of behaving in a way which divides us from the collective, the defense mechanism is indoctrinated to build mental resistance to deter us from doing so. The dilemma with culture nowadays being that, by implication, the population aspires to be mediocre with general as many individuals are reluctant to accept hardship to exit the bubble of security. Therefore, by succumbing to this social strain, we limit to the average and poor our successes and our satisfaction.

Human beings are social creatures and therefore most people want their friends to accept them and become part of the group. Nevertheless, we still need to search for what makes us as individuals fulfilled and happy. The ambitions only for fitness will never be lost or weakened. Nor would we authorize tradition or social pressure to affect our goals as this ensures that we essentially place our lives into the hands of others. We have only one life and every second we have less of it left! We have to make sure we live this life by ourselves as the only people we are all. In order to stay conservative, we can never doubt our ability or our hopes.

While a conventional thinking system has been around for eons, it's not the normal order of things. It is primarily all that we know during our lives from others. Tell a kid about four as they grow up what they want and stuff such as sports car drivers, astronauts, actresses, a supermodel, a boxer, a ballerina, etc. can be asked. Nevertheless, the vast number of children who leave school have significantly lowered their expectations and the rest are glad to have a career. Somewhere along the way we are convinced of the childishness of our initial expectations and of something more realistic and practical. Our modern views make us follow traditional professions and lifestyles (as in average).

My friend has always been really involved in motorsports. He was good enough for a racing team in his youth and spent time with engineers and drivers. He was so pleased with the rally that he decided he wanted his future to be in that line.

He had to go to see the professional trainer at his school when he was around fifteen years old. Once my friend was asked what he wanted to be, he responded happily that he would be a rally driver. He was quickly told by the job specialist that he was to look for something realistic, and then sent him a local factory application form. In less than five minutes the job coach persuaded my friend that being a rally driver was only an immature fantasy. My friend took the counselor's advice and applied to a local factory where he is still working. Her job pays for the bills, but he's never so happy that he's still very excited about working the field of motor racing.

I can't help my friend feel that when he was younger he should have told the careers advisor what he wanted to be. And if he responded to anything but a "career consultant," my friend was justified in saying that the life consultant may also not have been qualified to give advice because of the mess in his own career.

The truth is, people make a living racing cars. There is simply no reason why my friend should not have fulfilled his vision. The careers adviser should have told him to approach the relevant organizations. Speak to those who are employed in this field to see what advice they will offer. In the field of racing he had already formed connections and would be allowed to network more. Perhaps, through his attempts he might have had to get a day's work to pay bills. So maybe the jobs adviser urged him to see if he could become a mechanic and to see if he could have an apprenticeship with a rally car company, etc. Nevertheless, a job in the area where he works is seen as a great success in the local factory, which is why both the career adviser and my friend embraced conventional wisdom.

It gets more difficult to think critically as we grow older and indoctrinated into mediocre thought. We ought to disregard traditional wisdom in order to live truly happier life and be able to fight the world. Another essential feature of critical thinking is that it is able to describe precisely what success means to you. A big home, a lot of money and good stuff are included as a traditional image of performance. It's perfect if that's what you want out of life. We must also bear in mind, however, that achievement is neither the material resources nor the things we possess. And what's achievement? The greatest description of achievement I've heard is that of Christopher Morley, a prolific writer and editor, who said: "There's only one thing to do - so you should live your life to your own enjoyment." It is not the dream for success that prevails.

One guy I know really wanted to be a taxi driver. This was also his dream, as far as I can recall. Once asked what he was going to be when he grew up, the' bus driver' was still answered. Now it might seem to some as a strange ambition but his dream of achievement was to be able to drive buses for a career. Want to know where I've seen him last? He's been behind a bus handle! The dream had been fulfilled. His goal was simple and he left and achieved it. I'm sure in the mansions there are millionaires who're not close to this guy as satisfied. Success is just what we agree to be individually. When we pursue others ' dream of success, even though the goal is split into millions, we will never be satisfied! To order to construct our own dream of the ideal future, we must have the mental power.

It is necessary to free oneself from the limits of traditional wisdom in order to lead exceptional lives and do extraordinary things. Seek to find someone who is exceptionally popular from past or current who has not been considered divisive, revolting, crazy, unorthodox, unusual or special. Either I can't believe either! It suggests that a prerequisite for achievement is the autonomous and unorthodox form of thought. It takes bravery, as we have already said, to go against the crowd (thereby the crowd still takes action against you). Nonetheless, you should be confident, if you choose to be special, that while you are on less-traveled roads, it is a path that all the effective persons have taken.

Critical thought is definitely a form of death. Many that are able to believe openly frequently struggle to realize the significance of the challenge. The culture and schooling have fostered a similar way of thought. We watch the movies and Television shows, the magazines that we read and the songs we hear and the people who we meet all have an influence on the way we think.

We are bombarded with advertisements from the moment we get to sleep and continue to form our thoughts as well. All it takes for a celebrity to dress in any fashion, or to get a certain haircut, with ten thousands of people looking the same within a week. Citizens normally feel as they are expected to look, hope for the things they are told that they should get, listen to the music they are told to listen and express the views they are often allowed to read in the newspapers and magazines. A million different sources affect our way of thinking, and it can be impossible to distinguish our own views from the perceptions and perspectives of other sources. Independent thinking is rarely easy or quick.

This does not necessarily reject the common views and points of view to consider critically. Independent thinking is able to think for yourself, to challenge the existing wisdom independently to see if it's valid to you. Some individuals actually overturn the values of the moment, for example, when other individuals favor materialism, the radical accept faith. If atheism is popular a little longer, then materialism can be accepted by the revolutionaries. How others tend to understand is that they encourage the accepted views to influence their actions by merely changing the agreed views. True self-contained philosophy is the master of your own ideas.

Some people wrongly believe critical thought is dangerous. You think that living about yourself is bad for society, it contradicts existing values and is inherently egoistic. While these people may try to diminish the idea that they are special, the advance of our democratic civilization relies on critical thinkers! The culture will stagnate without anyone willing to shake the world, think "unreasonable" thoughts and criticize tradition. I think this idea is nothing more than George Bernard Shaw's terms ' the fair man adapts to the environment; the irrational man tries to try to conform the universe to himself.' Any advance therefore depends on the unreasonable guy.' He is the unreasonable thinker who has the potential to turn the universe! I might also go so far as to say that it is your duty to be' unreasonable' to society and to speak for yourself! Therefore, we lack the opportunity to see problems in certain ways and then come up with a new approach because we behave the same way as anyone else. Modern culture depends on critical thinking, which should be actively promoted, in order to advance.

The irony is always the worst when it comes to dismantling proven morals. An autonomous thinker does not deny existing values, but challenges them. Morality, which is not real, is under such pressure to crumble. Slavery, slave labor, religious control rights, and so forth, were all at once seen as religiously pure by the people! Yet just and fair values, which are more sense and importance, are justified by asking. The definitive reality is often accepted as a means of confirming and affirming the validity, challenging. Critical thought does not exclude individuals from moral obligations; it supports a social responsibility and enhances it.

This carries with it a tremendous commitment to critical thought. You have a growing obligation to yourself and others as a critical thinker. For your own opinions and the outcome, you are solely liable. Therefore, you are always accountable for how your acts impact you and others. This can often be tenting to let other people think about us. Understanding yourself needs commitment. The related responsibility may also be passed over to others. But this lack of ability to consider and take responsibility means that we lose power of our lives and our own fate.

Our emotions influence our actions, our actions are our habits and our habits form our characters, and our characters decide the lives that we lead. When we authorize others to speak about us, their opinions will decide our lives. My friend's career counselor claimed that a safe engineering job was more realistic than a rally car driver. My friend allowed the job counselor to dream about him, so he is now in a factory.

You are likely to feel the need to adapt, play it safely and embrace the traditional as you step into life that you want to lead. This wish is just another form of mental resilience we should go through and use to improve our minds. We have to make sure we think individually. We must describe our own dream of achievement clearly and then have the confidence and courage to avoid chasing the bandwagon and pursue the view. We must be free from all restrictions or limits and aspire to be special. We have to be able to be experimental, unorthodox and non-committal. Once we get rid of chains of common and day-to-day thinking, we know what we might all attain and what limitless opportunities life gives us if we are able to accept them.

FINANCIAL FREEDOM

Money makes the world go round. Hard earned cash pays the bills and a roof above your head. But capital is not growing on trees. You must get it. You must get it.

Clichés aside, it is valid that money is difficult to come by. You must work hard and extremely smart to get the green. And soon you will hit a peak, a limit – the limits of how much you earn. When you've struck, increasing the net worth once again would be challenging.

When you excel financially, you own the wealth more than you own it. The profits do not automatically decide how good you are financially – the decisions and goals. When you fail, financial achievement can appear as a distant vision, but you can make this dream a reality by following these ten steps:

- Establish Goals

- Take Stock of Your Current Financial Situation

- Create a Spending and Savings Plan
- Establish an Emergency Savings Fund
- Invest Diversely
- Make Sure You're Covered
- Establish a Good Credit History
- Delete Your Debt
- Buy a Home
- Seek Advice and Do Research

Step 1: Establish Goals

A crucial element of everybody's financial strategy is to identify simple, realistic goals. One financial goal is to include the same amount of money needed to purchase or deliver a particular service at a given date. Having the target realistic lets you decide how much you have to keep track of your success every month.

Three types of targets exist: short, mid and long ranges. Short-term targets must be reached in a year or less, in a mid-range span of one to five years and in five or more years. Typical short-term targets are holidays, presents and gadgets. A home down payment is a growing mid-range goal. Saving for retirement and further education of a child can be long-term priorities.

The chart of Financial Goals will help you decide your target time and the amount of money you would need to invest annually to meet your goals. Depending on the present financial condition, you can find the figures overwhelming or not even possible. You will be able to raise your revenue and/or lower your expenditures or have to consider changing your expectations. Completing measures 2 and 3 will allow you to assess how valid your expectations are.) It is necessary to decide your goals. Speak to somebody else and set goals together if you share your finances. It is not unusual for couples, without understanding something, to work financially at cross-purposes. This would be much easier to accomplish your goals through communicating by deciding what is most important.

Step 2: Take Stock of Your Current Financial Situation

The explanation of what you're in today's financial condition will help you decide tomorrow. Are you on the right road or require a change?

Net Worth

Assets are items of monetary worth that you possess. These can include homes, cars, mobilizations, investment checks and savings plans, bank certificates, mutual funds, inventories and bonds.

Monetary commitments to other individuals or corporations are liabilities. These liabilities include mortgages, auto loans, debt with a credit card, personal loans and student loans. Your savings are worth less than the liabilities. When your net worth is high, you have more than you owe. When your net worth is negative, you owe more than you own.

Your net worth is at one point in time an image of your finances. At least once a year it is a smart idea to measure your net worth. Over time, the net worth will increase. When it doesn't, you won't either earn enough or take too much of the mortgage. You will improve that by changing the spending and savings strategy.

Cash Flow

Do you know where your money goes every month precisely? You're not isolated, otherwise. Many of us are well aware of financial crisis signs such as defaults with credit cards, checkouts, unwilling, or late payment of bills, but are not clear about the cause. You will work it out by measuring the cash flow.

Cash inflows are income. The most popular source of earnings is job income, but it can include such factors as investment earnings, compensation for families, alimony, rental payments, government benefits, contributions, and self-employment or hobby profits. Although donations, funding for children and other public services are not necessarily taxable, certain wages are taxable. Once taxes are taken out, the total revenue is your income. After taxes are paid, your net income is your income.

Cash outflows are expenses. This can include important elements such as mortgages, leases, housing, education and activities that you want to spend on, for example piano lessons and holidays. Savings can also be called an expense – the money does not leave the pockets, so it is not used for such purposes.

For report the income and expenditures, use the cash flow worksheet. You may want to chart your everyday expenses and get as precise statistics as possible. It's a smart thing to watch it if the sales is erratic. To assess the monthly revenue and expenditures, calculate and divide by 12 the annual sum.

Step 3: Create a Spending and Savings Plan

It is high time to draw up a strategy to invest and save money after you have taken stock of the situation you are in. Your spending and saving plan will show your potential capital. How much are you going to waste on clothes? So how much are you going to pay into your savings fund? How much are you going to pay in the grocery shop?

Be mindful of the golden rule of money management when designing your plan: your expenditures should never surpass your revenue. Start the worksheet with Cash Flow. You need to make changes if you have negative cash flow. You may want to make adjustments even though the cash flow isn't negative. You may, for example, want to save more money than you now or decide to take your child to private school.

Think of opportunities to improve your profits and/or rising expenditures if necessary. Could you get a part-time work? Does your house rent a room?? Cut off your meal? Will you miss the mocha latte every day $4? For a more competitive cable bundle or turn off your phone online? Growing sales can be challenging, but most people can reduce any expenses. Evaluate frankly what is and what is not important. In the Cash Flow Worksheet, use the target per month section to list your expense and investment schedule.

And if you follow it your strategy is successful. Monitoring your expenses constantly will allow you to see where you can stop spending and in a certain group you have exceeded your cap. You can chart your expenditures using the Fritter Finder or the screen list. Many budget systems also track the spending and credit card purchase automatically and categorize it. Try not to be disappointed when you spend over one month. There's no one fine. Very ever, the strategy will need to be re-adjusted to make it more practical. For instance, you may not keep the expense of your food at $150 a month, but you may cut back on your shopping.

Step 4: Establish an Emergency Savings Fund

Will you be able to afford your bills for the coming months if you lost your job? You should pay for the repairs if your vehicle breaks down, without having it on your credit card? Unforeseen circumstances arise and it can be difficult to cope with them with those earning paychecks. They can save money, threaten shut-offs, vehicle repossession and/or eviction or foreclosure from their homes, or charge credit-card products and provide only short term relief.

The creation of an emergency savings plan gives the opportunity to pay for costs in the event of the catastrophic case. Economic analysts suggest that critical living costs be reduced for at least three to six months. Figure out how much you will pay every month before you hit your goal because you don't have your amount of savings already. As you do not know when you need the money, make sure it is deposited in an readily accessible account where no early withdrawal penalties apply. Typically a good option is a savings account.

This is easier to recycle if you do it automatically. You will be able to invest half of your paycheck into your bank account because you have a direct deposit from work. In fact, several financial institutions require you to periodically move funds from the checking account to your savings account on a periodic basis.

Step 5: Invest Diversely

You know where the emergency fund will be stored, but where should you put savings for certain purposes? Investment classes are three primary types:

Stock: An equity component is a proportion in shareholding of a corporation. In other words, you'd own one-millionth of the company if a company is split into one million shares and you owned one share. You will make money out of collecting distributions of dividends and sell the shares for more than you bought them. In the past, securities have been the longest-term gain. There are no promises, though, – one day you could value your stock more than you spent, the next day less.

Bonds: A bond represents a loan for the bondholder, a corporation or country, as a creditor. If companies decide to collect money, bonds are released. For addition, when you hold the bond, you obtain the principal, the par value, annually at the bond maturity and the interest. You will purchase a bond below, at or above its nutritional value depending on the demand. In general, bonds are in relation to cost and return for stocks and cash equivalents.

Cash equivalent: The currency equivalent is investments which can easily be converted to cash such as savings and checking accounts, deposit bonds, deposit account money market and the U.S. Treasury Bills. They tend to be low-risk, and you can lose less to no money you invest. It leads in poor returns on currency equivalents. It is safer to retain capital in cash equivalents for short-range purposes. When you are about to spend your capital, your main concern is not to risk your main investment. If you stock your inventory in six months, the stocks are likely to be less valuable if you sell them.

The value of your investment in six months is less of a problem for long-term targets than inflation, the average rise in the price of goods and services over the course of time. The capital yield is most far below the inflation rate, which means that if you keep the cash there, its value declines significantly with time. This is why it is good to put in stocks and bonds, which on average have higher income than currency, for a large amount of money you save for long-range purposes. There is a chance of a decrease in the valuation of your savings, but the longer the investment period the lower your risk. While inflation may be a problem for intermediate targets, because the duration is shorter, the investment options will be more cautious.

A safe way to reduce the risk of money loss is to diversify the savings. There are a variety of stocks, shares, and cash equivalents in a balanced portfolio. (It is always a smart idea to diversify into each kind of investment class, based on how far you are away from your goals and risk tolerance.) You will buy stocks, for example, from retail, software and financial services companies. One quick way to achieve diversity is to buy shares in a mutual fund. Capital is invested in a mutual fund from various creditors to buy various securities, shares and/or cash equivalents.

Profit from tax-delayed accounts if available. For instance, as retires are provided by the company, use 401(k) or 403(b) or create a conventional IRA or Roth IRA alone. You can use a Coverdell College Savings Account or fund 529 if you save for your child's higher education. All these accounts make your income tax-free. 401(k)s, 403(b)s and the traditional IRAs require tax-free donations while you are entitled to tax-free deductions from Roth IRAs, Coverdell Education Savings Fund, and Plans 529.

Step 6: Make Sure You're Covered

Things such as a serious injury, car crashes and house fire, even though you have savings, will place a serious burden on your financial well-being. The right level of insurance will shield you from the financial repercussions of certain life adversities.

Health Insurance - Everyone needs to have health insurance. Many employers provide their employees and their dependents with community health insurance. You will have to pay a percentage of the insurance premium, but in most situations you would pay significantly more than if you were to buy your own insurance package. What if you can't get a full package and you can't get an allowance from work? You may be covered by the Medicaid or State Social Care Plan if your salary falls below any cap, or if you are pregnant or injured. The purchase of comprehensive medical insurance is another choice. Health emergency benefits, including medications and appointments to hospitals, do not cover daily insurance expenses, nor cover critical care emergencies such as hospitalizations. The deductibles are normally high, but the premiums are small.

Disability Insurance - When you are working, disability

insurance is a smart choice, it covers part of your wages when you cannot work. There are two types of plans for disabilities, short-term compensation for just a brief time (usually six months or two years) and long-term insurance until the age of pension. The most relevant policy is long-term policy. You will be able to save on your spending if you are out of service just for a few weeks. Yet a short-term retirement program can be a aid if the spending of money on insurance is a challenge. Once you buy a scheme of your own, see what protections you have from employment.

Life Insurance - You will remember this if you have a wife, infant, parent or somebody else who depends on your support. Life insurances are not only to cover the incomes, they are also meant to replace programs. A woman who is in the home may choose to buy life insurance for child care if she fails, for example. Two simple life insurance forms are available: term and cash value. Period insurance is life insurance. For a defined amount of time, you pay the fee, and then after you expire does the insurance payout. Cash-value life insurance pays half of the premium and half of it goes through a retirement account. So long as you pay the fee, you will retain the scheme. The saving program may even be lent for the money or canceled and cash is returned. However, the premiums on life insurance at cash-value are typically higher and that might not be worth the costs because you do not expect life insurance to be required for the remainder of your life.

Auto Insurance - The regulation allows drivers to at least provide an insurance vehicle guarantee in most countries, and protects the compensation expenses to a certain degree should you harm an individual or property in your vehicle. If the vehicle is many years old and is of no use, it might be sufficient to cover responsibility. You may want full coverage insurance, even if your vehicle is newer. If you have a car loan, the borrower would possibly need this. In addition to liability, insurance usually includes medical bills, uninsured motorist safety, crash coverage (which pay for repair or maintenance costs related to accidents), and comprehensive coverage (which includes repair and replacement costs due to losses incurred by other causes, such as thefts or fires).

Homeowners Insurance - When the house includes a mortgage, the lender would most likely need protection from homeowners. And if you owe nothing on your home, it will be a serious mistake to cause the insurance to lapse. To most homeowners, their house is their greatest asset – a catastrophe could cause financial damage if there is no insurance cover. The insurance includes fire loss, burglary and liability provisions for domestic owners. Standard insurance plans for homes do not mitigate damages incurred by disasters or flooding. You may choose to buy an extra provision if you are in one region in which one of these is a problem.

Renters Insurance - Insurance for renters includes personal property loss and renters liabilities. This insurance is very expensive, especially in contrast to the costs of repairing all of your clothing, furnishings, appliances and other items if stolen or destroyed. Suppose your landlord's insurance doesn't compensate your expenses - it'll probably not compensate your expenses.

Step 7: Establish a Good Credit History

You can affect your life in many ways through your credit report and ratings. Getting a mortgage or car loan is generally simpler with good credit background, particularly one with a decent interest rate), rent an apartment, find jobs (many employers check credit reports), and getting low-cost insurance.

Your credit report records your financial behavior as the name suggests. Several forms of loans are available, including credit cards, store cards, personal loans, car loans, mortgages and student loans and loan lines. The credit record also covers litigations pertaining to securities, such as penalties, foreclosures, repossessions, debt, bankruptcies and expulsions. Your credit score is a calculated review of the facts found in your credit report, to calculate how much chance you don't payback. You must have equity to get a decent credit report and ranking. For the first time you don't have a credit background, it can be tough to get accepted for credit. What do you do in this Catch-22?

A protected credit card is a good choice for a lot of people to start (or reconstruct). You have to register the deduction that is held by the borrower if you do not make deposits using a safe credit card. The credit cap is typically smaller and the fees are high because it is generally easier to do than with regular credit cards. However, after one year or two of on-time payments, several borrowers are willing to change a stable credit card to a normal one.

Another choice is to ask a relative or family member with a strong loan or credit card background to file for you. Test for this sort of structure in particular. Not only will any late fees be wrongly represented on your credit report, but your co-signer will still show that. You would choose to apply for loans of your own for six months or one year.

It is really important to do it wisely until you have credit. Still pay on time and keep the account balance low, even credit cards. Lack of payments, especially to a point where accounts are forwarded to the collection agency (usually after 4-6 months of non-payment) and the payment of high balances can hurt your credit report and ratings. Even negative are repossessions, stereotypes, decisions and bankruptcy.

Step 8: Delete Your Debt

This is best that the credit cards will never be charged. You might, however, be able to manage the credit card, personal loan or other kind of debt. A mortgage will take not only a large portion of the profits per month, but also costs interest payments for thousands of dollars. On the other hand, the settlement of your debt will give you a sense of alleviation and more capital, like savings.

Two easy forms to speed redemption of debt are available. One is to raise the payments. The monthly costs are also very low. If that is what you spend, then it could be years before you get debt-free. You will raise more dollars by keeping the bonus fees in mind by consistently concentrating on a single-payer instead of giving a bit money to all the investors because you have several accounts. Most people want to start debiting with the lowest balance as it gets paid as soon as possible and offers incentive that can make it easier to keep going. (You can also make minimum payments to everybody, of course) You will also save more money by starting with the lowest interest rate of debt. When the first loan has been repaid, add the money to the loan with the next lowest balance (depending on the choice) or interest rate and so forth, before all the debt has been repaid.

You will lower the interest rates on the other way. You will get lower interest rates in a variety of ways, including:

- To urge investors to lower interest rates directly. If you have made deposits on time, investors will usually be more likely to do so. We might say no, of course, but it didn't hurt to inquire.

- Switch the balance to a low-interest rate card.

- Obtaining a credit for consolidation. This depends on your loan, wages, and current amount of debt, whether or not you get one.

- Paying down new domestic debts or loan or refinancing in cash (including refinancing your mortgage more than you owe). Generally the interest rate is smaller than on most other loan and the interest will be paid. This will also be borne in mind that, if you cannot afford your mortgage payments, you will lose your house.

- Participate in a repayment program that offers reduced rates of interest for investors to counsel and close accounts.

Remember if you are using leverage to bail off interest if you are talking about restructuring, mortgage loans, home equity sheets, or cash refinancing. You also increase the amount of debt rather than raising it as you continue to use and wear an equilibrium on old cards. Those options work better if you don't consider extra debt. All of these approaches are not mutually exclusive to accelerate debt repayments. This is also a smart idea to both increase your contributions and lower the interest rates.

Step 9: Buy a Home

It can be a very wise investment to buy a home. While the demand for real estate fluctuates, over time most homes gain value. Uncle Sam also subsidizes tax breaks on the property investment. When you sell your estate, you will be free from paying taxes for up to $250,000 ($500,000 for couples filing a joint marriage) on the income from the sale as long as your estate has served as your main residence for at least two of the next 5 years. You will subtract tax on the mortgage interest and property taxes on the refund, and when you sell your house

It's never too early to start dreaming as you think of buying your own house someday. A down deposit makes it much easier to secure a mortgage authorization, and if you may not have one, you will not be able to receive a mortgage. Whereas 20% of the purchase price was the necessary down payment, many borrowers today consider less. You can also have to purchase private home protection or get a higher interest rate on the second mortgage. This is a smart idea to save on closing charges (sales charges, such as attorney fees, title protection, appraisals, assessments, tax escrows) as well as on post-buying contingency funds in addition to down payment.

A good credit score and low debt ratio also assist in mortgage applications. A FICO score of at least 680 is required for approval by many mortgage lenders and for the best interest rate in the mid-700s. The smaller the mortgage, the greater the value of the loan you may demand. Most borrowers recommend you not surpass 36-38 percent of your gross income for your current loan contributions and your mortgage payment.

Homeownership isn't perfect for everyone. When you travel

about often or fail to meet your existing financial commitments, mortgage will pose only a burden. It is necessary to assess your financial commitments objectively to decide whether and how much you can afford to pay a loan. Do not necessarily depend on the lender's permission to tell you what you can spend – review your estimates carefully. You will not gain money because you accept a mortgage that you cannot keep up with and losing your house – it hurts your credit record only. If you agree that it is currently not a reasonable idea, you will still rethink owning a house in the future.

Step 10: Seek Advice and Do Research

Financial problems can be complex in a great deal of our lives. We typically know less about the financial accounting at school and get the most from our parents who may or may not have experience. When in certain aspects of personal finance you feel a little confused, contact a expert for help. Not knowing everything is not ashamed. After all, if you're a bad guy, go see a hospital, take him to a mechanic if the car breaks down. Turn to a financial advisor because it's just relevant.

Some of the kinds of financial professionals that you can seek assistance from include financial planners, securities counselors, credit counselors and insurance brokers. Most contractors are fair and legal, but not everyone. Speak to others to inquire for their credentials if you are looking for a consultant in a specific field.

Don't be afraid to listen to your intuition-if it gives you a negative feeling that's reason enough not to use it.

You should know on your own as well. The internet is rich with information, so take care of the origins – anyone should create a website. A professional financial advisor or Joe working in a doughnut shop on the street might be an investing story. There are a number of personal finance books and periodicals, all of which can be found in the library, meaning you don't even need to order them.

A constant cycle is an effective financial accounting. It is important to constantly track and change your schedule for your expenditures, savings and investments. Luckily, you don't have to be a personal finance professional to excel, so you can gain care of your finances with a good knowledge of the fundamentals-and follow these measures.

APPROACHING RISK

The inherent consequence of development is risk-taking. We have to step past our comfort zone to our growth area to make progress. It still sounds dangerous to leave the security zone behind. Therefore, if we want to go on, there is no way to escape the sense of fear. We never leave our comfort area or know our true capacity because we just play it safe.

The only way to avoid risks is to stop progress, and we who want to make progress need to analyze how we are faced with risks. The sense of danger is also understood to be a form of mental resistance, such that we cannot escape the zone of our safety. To conquer this psychological pressure, we use our emotional power to function positively. This constructive action strengthens us and thereby helps us to move forward. Yet the sensation of danger will still be so strong that we cannot resolve it. In this chapter, we shall look a bit more closely at the essence of the danger and how we have to cope with the risk if we want to go forward.

The first aspect we need to look at is why people fear danger because they know they are taking risks. Apart from the fact that the danger isn't particularly pleasant, another reason why people don't like to take risks is that most of us are not interested. So much were you willing to take a risk? Compare this statistic with the amount of times you were advised to be alert.

They are focused on not engaging in dangerous behaviors from a very early age. It is the best thing to do in many situations. A kid, for instance, must realize that it's unsafe to run on the ground, which is why it cannot be done and cautioned against. Nevertheless, there is a lot of contrast between the threats that can impair our well-being quickly and seriously, and the threats we encounter in order to lead lives that are fulfilling. Unfortunately, we sometimes compare the two and are programmed to view any danger as evil.

It is important to distinguish between risk-taking and recklessness to help us develop a deeper understanding of risk. When we act ruthlessly, we act blindly and impulsively. We have no strategy and no concern for the consequences of our actions. Reluctant action puts something in Lady's hands and the consequences can be devastating if we are miserable. In comparison, we have a strategy to help us cope with this challenge, when we take a gamble, in the way that gives us the greatest chance of success. We have looked at the choices closely. We have methodically prepared and determined that with reasonable odds of success we can take the risk. We take a calculated phase in our field of growth when we take a constructive chance. When we behave ruthlessly, we are lucky enough to have no measurable gain.

Between aggressive actions and constructive risk-taking, there is a significant difference. But, as we have already mentioned, the two appear to group together and many people are often discouraged from taking chances from their early years. While it is natural to warn them, as they strive to succeed in their lives, they should be motivated to take the constructive chances that they are continually facing. When we just play it comfortably, we are always in a comfortable spot, and we do not live a serious and less rewarding life by that.

They will now ensure they learn how to handle risks correctly and that we have established the distinctions between constructive risks and risky behavior. Every dangerous scenario is definitely unpleasant, but a good risk means that the construction environment is closely researched. We will never try to make such a major leap forward that we are overwhelmed in the field of growth. If we face a potential risk, we have to ensure that we prepare how we handle the danger so that we have the highest ability to implement our strategy effectively with the same degree of intellectual strength so abilities.

To abandon our comfort zone, it requires bravery. Always

equate bravery with ruthlessness, though. The implications of their actions are sometimes little to no known by a reckless person. Hence their acts are not bold or noble, but instead reckless and cruel. This is good to be scared so long as anxiety motivates us to brace ourselves properly and does not excuse remaining where we are.

To stay where we are is potentially far more of a challenge than to face fears on our path to our targets would eventually be. Many people live their life as if they are immortal, we mentioned in the previous chapters. You don't even realize that one day you will run out of time and die. They put things away and escape danger, because they still think they will do the stuff they want to do someday. The harsh and frustrating reality is that we all run out of time. We always get back to the end of our days, second to second. By not taking constructive steps to our goals, we face the exponentially greater chance that we will never live the lives we wish to lead! Once we realize also that our lives are extremely short, it is obviously the riskiest decision of all to play safely.

While seeking to escape any risk, we are sure that we do not live our lives in the way we want. Once you consider this, optimistic risk-taking doesn't seem like risky anymore, especially as compared to an alternate lifetime of cooperation and hope. From the correct point of view, constructive risk-taking does not seem to be too dangerous! Although certain people reject any threats and sometimes warn you against them, others that pursue their goals will not dread danger as they realize that this is a necessary aspect of development. While some pause and undo, the mentally strong just keep steadfast.

We will still prepare for and predict results because we are able to take risks. Nevertheless, we must always be mindful that we also have the possibility that events do not work as expected and that we have erroneously estimated them. Now I know some of you might think it was a little pessimistic for me to warn you that having used the last 1,000 words or so to persuade you of the rewards of taking chances, given your attempts something might be false! I'm sorry to be a killjoy if you feel that way, but it's a matter of fact that stuff do go wrong. No promise is ever made that events will always be specifically scheduled. Yet the psychologically healthy do not expect any promises or even like any!

The psychologically dominant realize that we are just at risk if we abandon our comfort zone. You must realize that in order to evolve, we have to step beyond our comfort zone. There will be no development if there is no feeling of fear. It is a sure sign that we are still comfortably inside the comfort area because we are expected to achieve success. If there is no chance, the job we do is not tax enough to lead us to rise. Through nature, if we really advance ourselves, we are above ourselves and taking a chance. It's a good risk, ideally, but it's still a risk. We're never going to move if we do not move until we have a promise of success! In order to develop, we must be willing to take risks.

While some want to sit where it is and wait for risk-free (that is not), some are able to take chances and advance. We need to be prepared to take chances and realize that when we get out of our comfort zone there are no promises of success. Paradoxically, the fact that we are able to act without assurances of success means that change is assured! Any time we face a challenge, we won't always succeed, but we will always be able to increase our mind, gain knowledge, and develop our talents.

We have not suffered as long as we know and develop from experience. We may not have fulfilled our immediate intent but we will learn, evolve from disappointment and become the kernel of our potential success if we sustain an optimistic mindset. The scientifically strong see all improved prospects.

When we risk and feel that we have not yet achieved the task, the experience will help us improve when appropriately managed so that we can be ready for the challenge in future. We have truly lost even if we stop trying.

We addressed the importance of continuity in this book earlier. When we have enough emotional energy, we know that all things are fine and that we follow our goals unremittingly. Regardless of the challenges and failures that we face, we are bound to evolve out of the comfort zone, and so the success of this development is almost expected. In the other hand, failure is assured only when we stop trying.

Danger is a crucial aspect of development to recapture. If we want to make change and live our lives, we need to be prepared to face the chance. We are rarely rudely behaving. In order to give us the greatest chance of success, we train and schedule carefully. However we know that when we get out of the comfort zone, there are no promises and we are not looking for fictitious change without risk. Because there are no promises, we understand that events will not necessarily go as we expected or wished to. Nevertheless, these mistakes are the seed to our long-term progress as we continue to continue to achieve our goals and use our short-term mistakes as a way to evolve.

The greatest risk is that we will not take the constructive risks contributing to growth and development. We are doomed to mediocre lives because we never take chances. A constructive approach to risk is a critical and necessary aspect to realize our true potential and to live happy life.

OPEN-MINDEDNESS

Open-mindedness can also be quite difficult. Most of us acquire a collection of religions and ideals and continue to be surrounded by individuals who hold the same ideals and convictions throughout our lives. It will also be challenging if we are faced with thoughts that contradict our own, because even though we may try to be open-minded, from time to time we will struggle with it.

I want to say that I am quite open, just like most people, I have some very strong convictions on some things and I find it difficult to manipulate those convictions — no matter how many people seek to convince me. Of course, I truly believe strong convictions can be wonderful and I think we can all be true to what we believe in, but it doesn't have to mean a closed mind to have strong beliefs.

While sometimes it can be hard to do, I also found that I had reaped a lot of rewarding rewards when I opened my eyes. There are many benefits to be made by opening your mind to fresh thoughts and fresh values. Here are just a handful of the advantages that I have found since I took the time to see the world around me.

Benefits of Being Open-Minded

Letting go of control. You free yourself from the full influence of your emotions when you open your mind. You will explore new concepts and opinions and doubt your views at present. To look at the universe with an open mind can be very empowering.

Experiencing changes. Opening your mind to fresh thoughts helps you to alter how you perceive and see the universe. Now this does not automatically mean that you can change your views, but if you consider with a rational mind, you have the choice.

Making yourself vulnerable. One of the most frightening (and biggest) aspects to see the world with an open mind leaves you weak. In deciding to be open-minded about the future, you admit that you don't always know and that you might not have worried of possibilities. This could be both terrifying and thrilling.

Making mistakes. This does not appear like committing errors will be a major plus, however it is. You allow yourself not only to notice possible mistakes, but also to make new mistakes as your mind is opened and you allow yourself to see it from the viewpoint of others. This doesn't seem like a lot of fun, but giving up and standing up again is a wonderful experience.

Strengthening yourself. Open-mindedness provides a forum on which you can create and pile up an idea. You will discover new concepts with an open mind, and expand upon the old ideas with the latest ideas. Everything you can do will bring together and affirm who you are and about what you believe. Without an open mind, it is very difficult to draw on observations.

Gaining confidence. You have a good sense of yourself when you live with an open mind. You are not limited to your own views or restricted to other people's values. That is why, when you know about the world around you, you will have faith and build respect. Openness helps you learn and develop and improve your self-confidence.

Being honest. There is an openness that goes with open-mindedness and to be open-minded means that you aren't all-knowing. It means that any truth you discover can still have more to it than you do. Such knowledge creates a sense of integrity within the character of someone living with an open mind.

Many people find it easy to be open-minded, almost as easy to breathe. To some, having an open mind may be a struggle, something they continue to learn and aspire to do. Whether you are open-minded or not, in the following list you can definitely see that living with an open mind has many benefits. It isn't always easy to do, but the opportunity to think freely and welcome new thoughts would be worth it, because you can be a witness to the rewards of opening your mind. It's not always easy.

INTENSE INTENT

There can be no growth without intention. Our thoughts are our feelings, and our thoughts are our actions. If something is to be done, then it must be our goal. The purpose is the first reason for any success and development. In almost any area we want, we will advance and grow talent. First of all, though, is the aim to promote and grow the talent. In doing so, we will find circumstances that improve our strengths and so allow us to achieve what we want.

Whatever sector in which you wish to excel, it is nothing to dream of, admire and long for. You will be able to do so. Desire and desire tend to passive emotions and thoughts. You don't give us anymore. However, the aim still leads to execution. True purpose is a cycle that cannot end. We wait to come to us when we want something. When we decide to do it, we're going out and we're doing something. Desire is a way to give in to the illusion of fate. Intention is an irresistible strategy of struggle which gives our lives power.

To be productive, we need to identify precisely what success is.

When we don't have a goal to aim for, we will surely miss. We will then determine how we reach our goal after we have established our purpose. To order to fulfill our dream of prosperity, we above all need a clear goal. Our goal must be white in color.

Throughout this book, we addressed the important and vital aspect of any success in overcoming anxiety, anger, self-doubt, and all other types of mind-resistance. We have find that it's not easy to meet mental opposition. Until we are ready to live with this pain, we will not be able to improve our mental strength and grow into our present comfort zone. By being stuck forever in our comfort zone, we do not live. We do not live. It is always difficult to move away from the comfort zone into the growth zone, and we therefore need some kind of propulsion to move us. This guiding power is the goal! The better our goal, the stronger the engine. Our aim must be as powerful as possible to ultimately achieve the goals we have set for ourselves.

No challenge would be too big to conquer if our motives are serious, if we have a clear determination to meet our targets. The force of our purpose will wash away all internal and emotional opposition. We are invincible if our goal is bigger than our obstacles.

You will definitely face emotional discomfort when moving away from your comfort zone. It will propel you through discomfort if your aim is good. Overcoming mental strength will improve your mind, build up your creativity and allow you to continue. Nevertheless, if the purpose is fairly low to accomplish your aims, it is impossible that you can get beyond the opposition of the mind. No challenge or inconvenience will hinder you if you really want it. Every effective person I know is committed to achieving their objectives.

I was far from sportingly talented as a child. I was one of the last to be picked for athletics at school and I was highly shy. I watched Bruce Lee's ' Inside the Dragon ' video at the age of 12, and became instantly intrigued with the martial arts. I was terrified of going to a dojo, but I decided to become a professional martial artist. Although I didn't know it at the moment, my emotional reluctance (fear, self-doubt) was a sure indication of losing my comfort zone and of changing myself. Yet as a young kid, my imagination flooded with a million people and one explanation why I wasn't allowed to go to the karate dojo any of my friends had attended. Fortunately, I had to conquer anxiety, self-doubt, etc. and needed to go to my first class. That was a positive thing.

I can recall perfectly the first time I walked into the dojo. Years later, I became the oldest teacher at the dojo, but I was completely terrified as an unathletic kid. The class didn't go well! It was the week before a graduation test and I needed to follow the best possible steps, as his interests lie with the students the next week. I totally ruined an experiment that caused the wind to pop me back. This was not enough for my wife to apologize. Once the professor picked me up, he told my husband not to apologize because I had not done as I was told (which was true). It was my own fault. If I wanted to quit, I left the dojo utterly disappointed and confused.

I was scared to come back for a whole week. Yet my goal was that I should return with all honesty. I did it, and I loved it! I loved it! The professor has more time to dedicate to me in my second class (I personally think he has spent more time with me than anyone else). I left the class with a wonderful feeling and look forward to the next lecture. I was always terrified before any lesson and it was years before anxiety started to fade, but my goal was to push me further.

My aim brought me from a scared and disheartened kid to a martial arts expert. As a kid, I was physically weak, but when I was there I wanted to be strong, I went and worked hard. The goal has made me better and better. I was also interested in a boy who wanted additional lessons to write to an author with several written publications and many published books. If you want to do it and that intention is strong enough, it's going to drive you forward, motivate you, and move you over challenges to make sure you reach your own goals. Nothing will deter you if you want it bad enough. When you are able to do whatever it takes to do it, you will do everything.

And as the first cause of every success is good intention, lack of intention triggers any mistake. Unless there is no goal, you will be overwhelmed by opposition along the way. You would definitely not face any opposition, and you can turn off what you would have been. As an instructor for martial arts, I have found many times that it is not the normal people that are farther apart but the best. Most men of the world slip by the road when they can't get any further and the time has come to venture out of their comfort zone. Many that have a clear goal proceed. In the martial arts there is a saying that a black band was a white band that could not resist. It is literally unlikely for you to stop if your goal is high enough! That's just not going to make the goal happen.

We know also why we want a particular goal and that awareness leads to ensuring that our goals are high. Let's assume that, for example, when you were a child your family never had a lot of money. That will help you make sure your family still has plenty of money. You are also committed to managing successful companies and never lose your children. Your goal will take you across any barrier. It's better than any emotional barrier or challenge you face to not see your family again. Completely knowing that we desire it should lead to a positive intention. Often, though, it's not easy to describe that we want to reach a particular goal, only because we want to.

I know that I want to work for myself: it's a deep sense of pride that comes from me. I was never successful at taking orders from someone and I think it's important to have freedom to enjoy my time on this planet. Any future employer's ambitions are impossible to suit my expectations, which is why I do not intend to go after them.

Tell me why I was still a novelist and I have no clue! I used to read and write, but I don't know why. Any psychologists might consider a cause, I'm sure, but to be frank, the explanation just doesn't matter to me. I know it makes me smile, and I want to compose powerfully.

You will continue to move ahead as long as your aim is high. I want to write clearly and so that's what I do. I have better expectations than the challenges I have been met by. I have faced these challenges with my goal, and therefore have grown intellectually and creative.

I love to compose. My intention to compose was therefore vital for my joy in life and my growth. Whatever is the underlying cause of your goal, it is vital for you to have this goal and to keep you walking in the growth zone.

Your goal will continue and keep you going while others stop. Purpose leads to practice, and practice leads to power and talent growing. You have a clear desire to proceed until you excel. Don't dream about things in your life you want: just intend them!

POSITIVE THINKING CAN HELP WITH MENTAL AND FINANCIAL GROWTH

Have you ever done a job you thought was overwhelming? Move back as far as you like to in your head. Perhaps it was as a kid because you knew you would never run faster than your best friend. Perhaps you felt that you never would get that driver's license as a teenager. And the moment at work that you felt that this wonderful idea would never be finished. Whether you have accomplished any of these goals, you have done them by setting expectations and taking a good approach-whether or not you know them.

This is the same approach to meeting the strategic goals. Although they can seem daunting or unattainable, the financial goals are entirely attainable. You will just need to develop a sequence of smaller steps to your target-so start today with step one.

Let's continue to smash the Steps.

How to Create a Positive Outlook

Attitude has been known to be all that makes a big difference. I couldn't agree more. Your mind is a factory of thought, and its ideas are your lifestyle actions. Build optimistic thinking and consider opportunities to accomplish your goals. Keep your feelings negative, and you will wallow in isolation. Here's how to build a positive perspective:

Become aware of your thoughts. Listen very carefully to that voice coming out of your head. When you believe, "I can get out of student loans" or "I can be a multi-billionaire," how does the voice react? If it says, "No you cannot, and here are a number of possible explanations," then you have at least a partly negative facility. That's all right; knowing that is the first phase to improvement.

Force your mind to think positively. Just as a real company can stop producing or start developing a new product, the mind can start generating optimistic thoughts. A good mental outlook questions if anything could be achieved instead of suggesting that it could not. Start by only looking for ways to tackle a problem. Your brain is very complex and knowledgeable, and inevitably, solutions will be found.

Speak positively. Do not be scared of telling them your goal if somebody asks what you are presently focused on in life. If they start giving you justifications as to why it is not possible, don't be scared to tell them that you're sorry they don't concur. You are going to have to benefit or suffer the repercussions of what you do today as this is your life.

www.ingramcontent.com/pod-product-compliance
Lightning Source LLC
Chambersburg PA
CBHW051538240526
45465CB00027B/686